Read a story that can help your career!

"…an excellent reference book that provides sound leadership principles."

> T. Michael Glenn, President and CEO
> FedEx Services

"Another insightful and inspiring work by David Cottrell. He brings home vividly what true leaders do for themselves and for others."

> Michael W. Grochowski
> Regional Commissioner
> Social Security Administration

"Never has mentoring been so needed; never has there been a book to fill the need like Monday Morning Leadership."

> Charlie "Tremendous" Jones
> Author of *Life is Tremendous*

"… a wonderful story sharing lessons of how to walk the leadership talk."

> Eric Harvey, President and CEO
> Walk the Talk Company

"Developing the eight principles in this book will immediately help you fulfill the responsibilities of your leadership position in the most effective way possible."

> Jack Kinder, Jr. and Garry D. Kinder
> Kinder Brothers International

MONDAY MORNING
LEADERSHIP

Inquiries regarding permission for use of the material contained in this book should be addressed to:
> CornerStone Leadership Institute
> P.O. Box 764087
> Dallas, Texas 75376
> 888-789-LEAD

Printed in the United States of America
ISBN: 0-9719424-3-9

Editors: Alice Adams
> Juli Baldwin
Book design: Defae Weaver
Cover design: Keith Crabtree

"… as insightful as it is concise. Its 'to the point' style provides a clear roadmap for becoming a better manager."
Dan Amos, Chairman and CEO
AFLAC, Incorporated

"… a practical, informative, step-by-step series of lessons packed with leadership techniques which are essential to success!
Ed Foreman
Executive Development Systems, Inc.
Former U.S. Congressman
Texas and New Mexico

"… presented in an entertaining and easy to retain format. Great book."
Ray Biggs, President and CEO
Security Finance Corporation

"A terrific guide on how to be a mentor and how to follow the advice of wise counsel."
Mark C. Layton, President and CEO
PFSweb, Incorporated

"… a wonderful journey with a mentor. It will help you achieve the success and happiness you desire. It's great!"
Brian Tracy
Author of *Maximum Achievement*

Other books by David Cottrell

MONDAY

MORNING

LEADERSHIP

8 Mentoring Sessions You Can't Afford to Miss

DAVID COTTRELL

CornerStone
Leadership Institute®

8 Mentoring Sessions You Can't Afford to Miss...

Prologue

Two Years Ago …

Things were not going well. For several years I had been a relatively successful manager for a Fortune 500 company, but now I was in a slump. I was working harder than I ever had, but I was going nowhere. I barely saw my kids. My marriage was suffering. My health was not the best. I was struggling in every part of my life.

At work, my team was also feeling the effects of my slump. People were upset. Business was slow — real slow — and the pressure on us to improve performance was rapidly hitting the "unbearable" level. To be honest, I was ready to give up, because my doubts about my leadership abilities were overwhelming the confidence I once had.

My questions outnumbered my answers. What if I wasn't the right person for a leadership position anymore? What if I had been successful in the past because of the great economy? What if I was just extremely lucky?

I was at a loss.

I was at the point where I needed to talk to someone — someone who would listen and offer suggestions without judging me.

One Saturday on the golf course, I saw a friend of my dad's named

Tony Pearce. Tony was a successful, semi-retired business leader who spent his time writing books and coaching top executives. I'm still not sure of his age. He looked only a few years older than I, but he was definitely light years ahead in experience.

Success had not changed Tony one iota. His warm personality, athletic good looks and charismatic personality were already legendary around our community.

Before his retirement, Tony was a "turnaround specialist," someone who was able to rescue companies from bankruptcy and lead them to profitability. He had been honored twice by various national organizations as "Entrepreneur of the Year" and was currently serving on a business council to develop a code of integrity for business executives.

During the course of his career, Tony had made millions. He was highly respected in the community because he gave so much of his time and money to help others. His integrity and ethics were above reproach.

My grandfather would have called him "a real gentleman." My father had the utmost respect for Tony and had often called upon him to serve as a sounding board during his own business career.

Tony was the type of person I aspired to be — wise, respected, confident and a highly sought-after speaker and mentor. But right now I was a long way from becoming the person I wanted to be.

When I graduated from college, Tony wrote me a congratulatory note that — for some unknown reason — I never threw away:

TONY PEARCE

Dear Jeff,

Congratulations on your graduation from college. You have completed a wonderful period of your life.

Now the learning really begins. I know you will be successful in the field that you choose.

If you ever want to talk about personal or business issues, I would be honored to allow you to learn from my experiences. . .you just have to ask.

Best wishes,

Tony Pearce

Tony had not seen me at the golf course, and it had been a few years since we had talked. I wondered if he would even remember me if I called him. I also wondered if he would take the time to meet with me since he was in such high demand by executives of major corporations all over the country.

After debating whether or not to call him, I finally decided that I had nothing to lose. My life was careening out of control and something needed to change.

I made the call.

A little nervous as I dialed Tony's number, I also was afraid that he wouldn't remember me and there I'd be…feeling like a fool. Even if he did remember me, a few years had gone by and a lot had changed since he had sent me that note. Maybe his offer was no longer on the table.

When he answered the phone, it only took a few seconds for my nerves to settle down and my fear to disappear. As soon as I said "This is Jeff Walters," he immediately knew who I was. He asked how Mom was doing since Dad passed away, and then he said he was honored that I would call.

I found it ironic that he used the same word — honored — that he had used in my graduation letter years ago. "What a coincidence," I remember thinking after we had finished our conversation.

After some catching up, I reminded Tony of his note from several years ago. I told him I was having some challenges at work and that I would like his advice…if he was still willing to talk with me.

After explaining some of the problems I was encountering, he agreed to work with me only if I would commit to two things:

1. Tony said that he was not interested in helping me solve my problems. He was interested in helping me become a better person and leader and that would require spending some significant time together. If I would commit to meeting with him every Monday morning for eight weeks, he would be glad to help.

2. Tony also asked me to commit to teach others the lessons and experiences that he would be sharing with me. He said none of my problems were unique and that others could learn from my experiences.

I was elated Tony consented to work with me, one-on-one, for eight weeks. I asked if we could meet on Fridays instead of Mondays, but he said his schedule would not allow that. So, I agreed to both of his requirements. "After all," I rationalized, "if the Monday Morning Meetings don't go well, I can somehow gracefully bow out of the rest of the sessions."

As it turned out, those eight meetings — my "Monday Mornings with Tony" — were the best meetings I have attended in my life. The thought of "gracefully bowing out of the sessions" never again crossed my mind.

As far as my second commitment — to teach others — that is my reason for writing this book.

I am honored you are investing your time in reading "Monday Morning Leadership" and ask you, in turn, to teach others the wisdom Tony shared with me.

Enjoy the journey, apply what you learn, and continue to grow as you share my Monday mornings with Tony.

The First Monday
Drivers and Passengers

 It was a rainy, gloomy day when I left home for my first meeting with Tony.

Frankly, I was somewhat cynical about whether meeting with Tony would really change things at work. At best, time with Tony would probably make me feel better about how things were going. I guess I really doubted he could do much to change how I managed. After all, I had worked for years for one of the best companies in the world and had been to numerous management development sessions. To no one's surprise, the impact of these highly-touted training sessions never lasted more than a short time.

I had to keep reminding myself — if things were great, I would have never called Tony in the first place. The truth was this: I was at a crossroads in my career. Deep down I knew that something was going to have to change, one way or another. "Get with it," I chided myself. "Executives all over the country ask for Tony's counsel. You should consider yourself fortunate he has time to talk with you."

We had agreed to meet at 8:30. Because of the rain, I drove into Tony's driveway at 8:40. Tony was waiting for me at the door, looking like he just stepped out of *Gentlemen's Quarterly*.

"Hello, Jeff. Welcome!" he said, extending his hand and pulling me toward him for a fatherly hug. "I am honored that you would take your time to come and see me."

Tony asked me to come in and gave me a quick tour. His home was incredible. It was large but had a warm feel to it. After the tour, he took me to his library where he said we would be meeting for the next eight weeks.

There must have been over a thousand books on his library shelves. I noticed several pictures of Tony standing with well-known business leaders I immediately recognized. Some of the pictures were taken in the library where I was sitting. I must admit I was a little intimidated.

After several minutes of catching up, he said it was time to get down to business.

"Your time is valuable, Jeff," he began. "I think we need to set some ground rules for us to follow if we're going to make the best use of our meetings; so I took the liberty of drawing these up while I was thinking about our sessions. See what you think."

He pushed a handwritten note across the table to me that listed three simple rules:

TONY PEARCE

Ground Rules for Monday Morning Meetings:

✓ *Start and finish on time.*
✓ *Tell the truth.*
✓ *Try something different.*

"Simple enough," I thought. "I can live with those rules." Then I looked back at Tony. "I can handle these. Let's get going."

"Okay then," Tony said. "Tell me what brings you here after all this time."

For the next hour, I did the talking and Tony listened without saying much.

I began at my college graduation, the last time we had spoken to each other. I had been so excited about the future; I felt there was nothing that would keep me from being successful. I was educated, energetic and full of optimism.

For the first few years of my career, success came easily and promotions were rapid. I worked in sales for one of the most respected technology manufacturing companies in the world.

Then I was promoted into management — my first big break — and I loved it. Business was good. I went on great trips. I was involved in making some big decisions, and I learned a lot, early on. My team was not top performing, but our results were acceptable, even more than acceptable.

Some of the people on my team didn't have the drive that I had, but business was so good that I didn't worry about them. Actually, I probably ignored some performance issues that contributed to the problems I had now.

Oh, and I tried really hard to be "one of the guys." I wanted my team to like me so they would *want* to work for me. So I frequently took them out for dinner and drinks — even shared some of the issues I was facing. At the time, it seemed like a good strategy.

About that same time, I believed the job upper management was doing was far from acceptable. In fact, I even told my team that if we did our jobs like upper management did theirs, our company would go under. We all laughed about that.

Those were the good times. But over the next several years, business began getting tougher. Most of my team was still intact, but some of the performance issues I once ignored were now affecting my division's performance in a big way — and by "big," I mean they were becoming threats to my job.

I was working hard — long hours — but the business indicators were telling me things were pretty bad. I wasn't very happy and the people on my team weren't happy. Our results reflected our frustrations.

"I looked you up, Tony, so I could learn from you," I said dejectedly. "I'm at my wits' end, and I hope it's not too late for me to turn this ship around."

He had listened for almost an hour when Tony finally started talking.

"First," he said, "I know you think these problems and the situation you described only exist on your team. You could not be more wrong. There are few — very few, if any — leaders who have not been faced with the same issues you've just shared. I know I have.

"When it comes to leading people, there is no problem that is unique to you. You could ask anyone with experience, and you would discover they have had to face the same issues, the same frustrations. So don't feel sorry for yourself. That's a waste of valuable time. Just make plans to make things better.

"Second, it's not too late to change," Tony continued. "You're still a young person even though you have a wealth of experience. I admire you for calling me and seeking advice. Few people have the courage to take that step.

"Obviously, you're facing some real challenges. Seeking an outsider's advice is a good move. We all need people who will help us look at situations from a different perspective," Tony said, his tone riveting my attention to every word. "In fact I have several people who are my mentors — people who have helped me gain new insights — and who have remained my mentors after all these years. It's not too late to change, but you will have to work to make improvements.

"Remember: You're not alone here. Most people have difficulty making the transition from employee to manager and from manager to leader. Your dad once told me something that I will never forget. He said that if you want to be extraordinary, the first thing you have to do is stop being ordinary. Wanting to be liked and 'just one of the guys' is natural. Of course, everyone likes to be liked. But as a leader, your team should like, or respect, you for the right reasons.

"If they like you because you're fair, consistent, empathetic, or a positive person — that's great. But if they like you just because you provide them with free dinners and drinks, what have you gained? You're setting yourself up for failure somewhere along the way. If your goal is to get everyone to like you, you will avoid making tough decisions because of your fear of upsetting your 'friends.'

"Transitioning from employee to manager or manager to leader requires that you make different decisions. And believe me, those transitions can sometimes create challenges in every other area of your life as well.

"I remember when you were a teenager, Jeff. You were so excited when you celebrated your 16th birthday and got your driver's license. Remember? You had watched your mom and dad drive for years, and as soon as you were old enough, you went through the driver's education course.

"Now, remember how confident you were? You knew that you would be the best driver ever. You even promised your dad with those very words," Tony said with a wink.

"Of course I do," I replied. "I also remember the second day after getting my license, I had an accident. Thankfully no one was hurt."

"I remember that, too," Tony nodded. "Most of your soccer team was in the car with you. But, what you don't know is that a few days later, your dad and I discussed that the main reason for the accident was your failure to understand the difference in responsibilities between being the driver and being a passenger.

"You see, passengers are free to do a lot of things the driver can't do. As a driver, your focus needs to be on the road and not on the distractions. As a driver, you no longer have the right to 'mess around' — like listening to loud music — even though it seems okay to do that as a passenger.

"The same principle applies when you become a leader. You're no longer a passenger; you become the driver. Even though your responsibilities increase when you become a manager, you lose some of the rights or freedoms you may have enjoyed in the past.

"For instance," Tony continued, "if you want to be successful as a leader, you don't have the right to join employee 'pity parties' and talk about upper management. You lose the right to blame others for a problem in your department when you are a manager and leader. You are the person responsible for everything that happens in your department, and that can be pretty hard to swallow."

But he wasn't through. "You even lose the right to some of your time because you're responsible for other people's time as well as your own," he said, stopping to check his watch. "Speaking of time, what time did you arrive today?"

"A little after 8:30," I said innocently.

"And what time did we agree to begin?" Tony wondered aloud.

"Eight-thirty. But it was raining, and traffic was heavy, and I thought I left in plenty of time," I stumbled.

"Yes, it was raining," he easily agreed. "But the rain didn't make you late. You see, Jeff, when you accept total responsibility for whatever happens, you make adjustments. When it's raining, you leave earlier, or take a different route, or call and change the meeting time. *You* control if you are on time or not. The rain just forces you to make different decisions.

"The opposite of accepting responsibility is to find someone or something to blame for the issues you're facing. Of course, there is always someone or something to blame, but a real leader spends his time fixing the problem instead of finding who to blame.

"What happens when you place blame is that you focus on the past. When you accept responsibility, you focus on this time forward — on the future. And Jeff, until you accept total responsibility — no matter what — you won't be able to put plans in place to accomplish your goals.

"One of the first things I want you to understand is that you have control over how you react to situations. If you eliminate blame — don't even have the word in your vocabulary — then you can make some positive changes."

Tony glanced at his watch again. "Well, I see we're about out of time today...as we agreed."

He handed me a blue spiral notebook with the words *"Monday Mornings with Tony"* handwritten across the cover. "Take this notebook and begin writing down what we discuss," he said. "It will be easier for you to keep track of when you need to review our discussions."

Tony stood and walked me to the door. "So is there anything you will do this week to make your situation better?"

"Well, what you said about taking responsibility makes sense, but there are so many external factors working on my team, I'm not so sure I can 'belly up to the total responsibility bar,'" I said sheepishly.

"But what I can do, for sure, is not participate in the pity parties or blame upper management for our problems. And I will try to take responsibility for everything and see how it goes," I promised.

"Write those things in the notebook when you get home," Tony suggested. "And remember, when you write things down, you commit to doing them. If you simply tell me what you want to do, there is really no commitment to getting it done."

I agreed and told him I would be there at 8:30 sharp next Monday.

I left Tony, feeling even more frustrated. It was going to be pretty hard to accept responsibility for everything that happened in my department, and I wasn't sure it was realistic. Some of the things he had said made sense, but were his philosophies up to date, I wondered. But, I had promised. I would try something different and then wait to see what would happen.

Later that day, I opened the notebook to record the lessons I had learned. Inside the notebook was a letter from Tony that read:

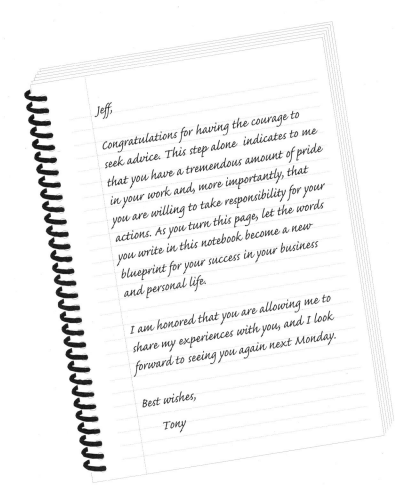

Jeff,

Congratulations for having the courage to seek advice. This step alone indicates to me that you have a tremendous amount of pride in your work and, more importantly, that you are willing to take responsibility for your actions. As you turn this page, let the words you write in this notebook become a new blueprint for your success in your business and personal life.

I am honored that you are allowing me to share my experiences with you, and I look forward to seeing you again next Monday.

Best wishes,

Tony

As I read the note, I could feel the genuineness of his words. He sincerely wanted me to be successful. And I began to feel more confident than I had in years that change for the good was on the horizon.

BE A DRIVER:

✓ Until you accept total responsibility — no matter what — you will not be able to put plans in place to accomplish your goals.

✓ Transitioning from manager to leader requires that you make different decisions.

The Second Monday
Keep the Main Thing
the Main Thing

 I drove into Tony's driveway at 8:20. It was pouring down rain again, and I waited for a couple of minutes before I dashed toward Tony's house.

He smiled as he opened the door just ahead of my swift trot into his foyer.

"Welcome," he said. "And good job! You made it with time to spare, and the weather is much worse than last week. Thanks for coming to my home, Jeff!

"And it looks like you learned something about responsibility last week since you made some different decisions that allowed you to be here on time today," he added with a smile.

"Yes," I agreed. "I learned to leave home earlier, but I'm not sure I did very well with my people, Tony. I tried to accept total responsibility for everything happening in my department, but the rats won the race again this week. Honestly, I have so many things coming at me from so many different directions, it's hard for me to get anything done…I mean done well."

"Tell me more," he said, settling into a comfortable winged-back chair.

"Well, I have fifteen people reporting to me," I began. "I also have two open positions. Karen, my boss, is demanding — and that's putting it mildly! I'm confident all my people know what they're supposed to be doing, but we seem to get less and less accomplished. We've spread out the responsibilities of the open positions to everyone on the team, but as soon as we put out one fire, another one pops up."

As I continued to speak, Tony seemed to become agitated and restless. "Are you okay?" I asked.

"Well, Jeff, it appears to me that everything is a crisis to you," he said. "Your job is not crisis management, and your people should not be firefighters. That said, I think there are some basic questions that require answers at this point:

- ✓ Why do you have two open positions?
- ✓ Why did these team members leave?
- ✓ Why do you think everyone on your team knows what they're supposed to be doing if they're not doing it?
- ✓ What are your priorities?

"Wait. Don't answer those questions now," Tony said. "Just think about them before next week.

"Now, let me tell you about one of my experiences," he continued. "I once worked with a manager who would remind us daily to 'keep the main thing the main thing.' The 'main thing' was our purpose or priority. Then he would ask us, 'So, what is the main thing?' And because every person on our team knew the main thing, this helped us focus on what was important.

"Actually, the main thing was really three things:

✓ Equip our employees with the tools to be successful.
✓ Provide outstanding service to our customers.
✓ Make a profit.

"If someone asked us to do something that was not part of our main thing, our manager would support us when we said that we couldn't get it done. We were a focused and productive workgroup because there was a clear understanding of our purpose."

Then he paused to let that sink in before he continued our meeting. "You mentioned that your people know what to do. Why don't you ask them, 'What is the main thing?' They probably have different perceptions of what the main thing is.

"I have found that when you depend on another's perceptions to match your expectations, you're setting yourself up for disappointment. Ask some questions…you may be surprised by your team members' answers.

"We'll spend another Monday on the importance of hiring the right people for your team; but now, I think you should try to understand why people chose to leave your team. It's a natural tendency (but not an accurate perception) to blame pay, benefits, upper management, salary administration, and other factors for someone's resignation.

"Now listen carefully because I want this to be very clear: People normally don't leave because of those reasons. People leave because their manager is not meeting their needs. People quit people before they quit companies. I'm not saying that's the case here; however, I am saying that in most instances the boss is the principal reason people resign.

"Speaking of bosses, you said Karen is a demanding boss. That's not a bad thing necessarily. I've heard many bosses called much worse. So how would you describe your relationship with Karen?"

"Well, that's just it. We really don't have much of a relationship. We have monthly meetings and that's about it. Karen is demanding because she's extremely results focused and is always requesting reports and information. I think she tends to get in our way."

"What are your expectations of Karen?" Tony asked.

"I think she should be a better leader. She should take the time to meet with me, provide recognition for my team, communicate with me, and help me be better at my job. After all, she's supposed to be my mentor. She doesn't do any of that — she's only interested in reports and results."

"Jeff, you're probably right. Maybe she should do a better job in those areas. Regardless, you still have fifteen people who are depending on you to develop a positive relationship with Karen. Your job is to inform her about what is going on in your department and achieve results. These are not options. For you to be successful and provide your employees with the necessary tools for them to be successful, you and your boss must work together — no matter what.

"I can understand why you think it's Karen's responsibility to develop a positive relationship with you — and you're right. However, if it's not happening, it's up to you to make some changes to make it happen.

"I suggest that you take the time to manage your boss the same way you manage your subordinates. Find out specifically what she needs from you and tell her specifically what you need from her. Do you know what her main things are? Does she know what your main things are? It may be worth a meeting to understand what both of you can do to help each other accomplish your main things.

"Okay, Jeff. Our time is about over for this week's meeting; so what are you going to do differently before next Monday?" Tony asked.

"Clearly, I think you're right about my team not knowing what the main thing is," I volunteered. "In fact, I'm not sure *I* know what the main thing is myself. So, my first job is to figure out what the main thing is and have a meeting to discuss it with the team.

"I will also try to meet with Karen to find out what I can do to help her accomplish her main thing. I will work on developing a positive relationship with her as best I can.

"I know we need more focus," I added. "I've let the circumstances dictate our actions rather than our mission dictating our actions.

"I'm also going to try to answer your questions. I have to admit I really don't think that I have two open positions because of me, but I will open my mind to that possibility," I concluded as we walked from the room.

As I left Tony's house, I couldn't get his words out of my mind: "What is the main thing? Why did two people resign? Why do you have all these fire drills?"

I had some work to do before the next Monday Meeting.

WHAT IS THE MAIN THING?

✓ People have different perceptions of what the main thing is.

✓ People quit people before they quit companies.

The Third Monday
Escape from Management Land

 "Good morning, Jeff."

Tony met me at the door for our third Monday Morning Meeting, looking as fresh and as dapper as ever. "You're on time and appear to be in a much better mood this week. I hope things are getting a little better at work."

"Well, I spent a lot of time on the three questions that I left here with last week," I said. "Much of my frustration has been not knowing what the problem was — much less what to do to fix it. I think I've made some real progress this week.

"First, I tackled the resignation issue head-on. I reviewed Jeni's and Chad's exit interviews. They both resigned during the past couple of months. And, just as I expected, the exit interviews didn't reveal much information. In fact, if you read each of the exit interviews without knowing what they were, you'd think both employees were happy to be working here.

"Taking my search a step further, I talked to a few people on my team. And while they were reluctant to speak for their former teammates at first, one person — Michael — provided some interesting information," I reported.

"Michael said neither Jeni nor Chad really wanted to leave, but they were unhappy about things that had been going on in the company. Michael also reminded me both Jeni and Chad received increases in pay shortly before their resignations, so pay had little to do with their decisions to leave.

"Your words from last week kept ringing in my ears: 'People normally quit because their manager is not meeting their needs. People quit people before they quit companies.' Well, I still felt some circumstance was the reason they left — not me or something I did," I admitted. "But I knew you wouldn't buy that answer, so I went to see both Chad and Jeni.

"I met with each of them individually, and since they no longer work for me, there was no reason for them not to tell the truth. I'll say up front, both seemed surprised I was interested enough to go see them, and they opened up — more than I expected.

"I was shocked by what I heard. Well, they didn't come right out and say it, but I left knowing that they didn't leave the company; they left me — their manager. Just as you said, I wasn't meeting their needs. So during my visit with each of them, I took a lot of time trying to understand what needs I hadn't meet. Basically it came down to three things:

"**First, hire good employees.** Their perception was I had gotten lazy in my hiring. In fact, one of them said that if a person could 'fog a mirror,' I would select them for our team.

"The problem was my good employees were being asked to do more and more, while others were being asked to do less and less. Chad even said, 'Some of us felt abused because we were good employees.' Honestly, Tony, I couldn't believe what they were saying. Could I really be punishing the good employees by giving them more work and rewarding the lower performing employees by allowing them to do less? Both Chad and Jeni thought so…and thought so enough to leave.

"Second, coach every member of the team to become better. I walked away from both meetings upset with myself. I hadn't provided adequate feedback and direction to either of these employees, employees I considered among my best. Really, I assumed — I know what they say about assuming anything — they were happy working without much feedback. I think I let them down by not paying enough attention to their individual needs.

"And third, dehire the people who aren't carrying their share of the load. I told you before about performance issues I had ignored. Well, those performance issues had an effect on the rest of the team. Jeni said what began as one negative and cynical employee became a whole team of negative and cynical employees. She said they kept looking to me to fix the problem, but I allowed it to go on…I did nothing.

"Needless to say, Tony, I was humbled after my meetings with Chad and Jeni. I was also a little relieved. At least I now know there are things I can do to avoid losing more good employees.

"I combined the other two questions you asked me to address into one: What is the main thing — the main purpose for our team?

"Wednesday, I had a meeting with my team. I prepared a paper for each team member to complete. On the paper was one sentence:

'The main thing in our department is…' and each person was asked to fill in the blank.

"Well, I know you won't be surprised by their answers, and really, neither was I. No one knew what the main thing was. Oh, everyone had an answer, but there was no consistency. This exercise showed me that instead of clearly defined goals and expectations, we had mass confusion about our most important mission as a team.

"So now I know our team has some work to do to define and understand the main thing. But, it seemed as though everyone felt good about having some direction established.

"I also had a good meeting with Karen. I think she appreciated me taking the initiative to meet with her. We still have a way to go, but I'm making it a priority to manage that relationship better.

"And yeah — I am in a better mood this week. I've realized there are things that I control that have contributed to my frustrations and the team's frustrations. Even though last week was not an ego-builder because of some of the answers I received, I do feel better. Now I know there is something that can be done, and it's something *I* can do," I confessed.

"Wonderful!" Tony exclaimed, although without surprise. "You made some great strides this week and I'm proud of you. But it sounds like one of the things you discovered is that one of the 'main things' for a leader is to eliminate confusion. We will talk later on about confusion — which can paralyze your team — but you've taken a giant step by working with your team to figure out what the main things are in your department."

My mentor continued, obviously pleased with my report this Monday. "Something that may have contributed to the confusion on the team is a trap many managers fall into," he said. "This trap is what I call 'management land,' where things are not always as they seem. And there's something else about this place — sometimes it's difficult to escape management land.

"In management land, simple things often become complex and people easily lose perspective. Managers begin to think the games others play are what are most important.

"In management land, people are rewarded for saying only the things managers want to hear. Egos are big and it's difficult to discover the truth. Management land can be described as confusing, frustrating and sometimes comical to those on the outside.

"What you learned this week is that you have to escape from management land and get in touch with your people. Chad and Jeni were right on the mark when they said that their expectations of you were simple: hire good people, coach everyone to become better, and dehire the ones who don't pull their share of the load. Jeff, their expectations actually translate into great advice!

"Let's look at it this way. On most teams there are three types of employees. Some are superstars — people who have the experience, knowledge and desire to be the very best at their jobs. Others are middle stars — they may not have the experience to be a superstar yet. Or maybe they are former superstars who for some reason lost their motivation to be the best. And then there are those I call falling stars. Those are the ones who are doing as little as they can get away with.

"A typical team has about 30% superstars, 50% middle stars and 20% falling stars. If you keep piling more work on your superstars — like Chad and Jeni suggested you had done — then you shouldn't expect them to continue to be superstars. Oh sure, some superstars will always be superstars regardless of the workload; but others will be beaten down into middle stars because of the additional work you pile on.

"Let's take a look at this chart:

TONY PEARCE

30%	Superstars
50%	Middle Stars
20%	Falling Stars

"Where is the minimum acceptable level of performance represented on this chart?

"Of course!" I said. "That's pretty simple. The minimum acceptable performance is in the middle of the 50%. Right here."

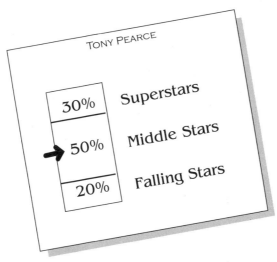

"No, Jeff. The minimum acceptable performance is actually here, at the bottom of the 20%," Tony corrected.

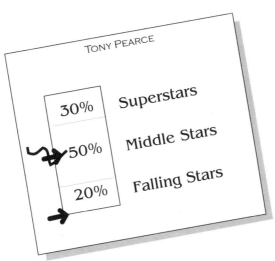

"You see, the people at the very bottom of the chart are still on your team, so their behavior must be acceptable to you. In fact, many managers — and you probably know some of these people — actually reward their falling stars by giving them less work while acknowledging them with decent performance reviews!

"When you do that, you should expect more people to fall into that category. Why not do less when there are still rewards?

"Your job is not to lower the bottom by adjusting for and accommodating the lowest performing employees. You should be raising the top by recognizing and rewarding superstar behaviors!

"You simply *cannot* ignore performance issues and expect your superstars to stick around for very long," Tony was emphatic about this point. "That's what Chad and Jeni were telling you. They said they needed you to coach everyone on the team and to dehire those who didn't carry their share of the load.

"I want you to try this. Write in your spiral notebook the name of each team member and then categorize them as superstars, middle stars or falling stars. And include Jeni and Chad as well."

"That's pretty easy," I said. "I definitely know my superstars and falling stars. I guess everyone else is a middle star. So, I've identified six superstars, including Jeni and Chad. Three team members are falling stars and eight are middle stars."

"Okay," said Tony. "Now I want you to take that back to your office, go to your files, and retrieve every person's most recent performance review. Then, put their most recent performance review score next to their name. Next, pull their personnel file. Beside each name, note each time that you've documented some kind of recognition or performance improvement over the past six months. It could be a letter of appreciation or a performance improvement document. Please bring that sheet with you next week.

"Well, once again, we're out of time, Jeff. But you're making some great progress, and I appreciate you taking our sessions seriously," Tony said with a smile. "Oh, and by the way, I am enjoying my time with you as well. So tell me, what are you going to do before we meet next week?"

"Well, I'm going to focus on several things," I began. "First, I will complete the superstars, middle stars and falling stars exercise…that may be interesting. Second, I will continue my team's discussion on identifying the 'main things' so we can begin eliminating confusion. Third, I'm going to work with human resources to start interviewing to fill the positions that are open. And finally, I'll begin the process of coaching my employees. But I need your help in this area — I'm not sure exactly how to do that."

"Great! You've got some work to do. And it sounds like you've already started thinking about our next meeting. I will be honored to help you on the coaching part — we can work on that next week."

"See you next week!"

GET OUT OF MANAGEMENT LAND

✓ Get in touch with your people

✓ Your job is not to lower the bottom by adjusting and accommodating the falling stars. You should be raising the top by recognizing and rewarding superstar behaviors.

The Fourth Monday
The "Do Right" Rule

 I arrived at Tony's house before 8 a.m. for our fourth meeting.

"Jeff, come on in. What brings you here so early?"

"I have a major issue that I need to talk to you about, and I was hoping we could meet a little longer today," I began, hoping my words were making sense and weren't as garbled as I thought they sounded. "I've hardly slept all weekend, and I really need your advice, Tony."

"No problem. Let me get us some coffee and we can get started." Tony swiftly returned with two steaming mugs of fresh coffee, settled into his winged-back chair and said, "Okay. What's up?"

"I feel like I took some quantum leaps backward since last week," I said. "I completed the superstar, middle star, and falling star exercise and found I had been really inconsistent in how I evaluated my employees. Some of my falling stars actually had better performance reviews than my superstars. I also checked the personnel files, though I already knew what was there — or should I say *wasn't* there. There were no letters of recognition and only one performance improvement documented over the past six months, and it was on a superstar.

"The bottom line is — I've lumped everyone into the middle as far as recognition and performance improvement. No wonder Jeni and Chad felt abused!" Now I was on a roll. "Discovering what I've been doing is disgusting. I should have known better. Actually, I did know better, but I did it anyway."

I took a sip of coffee. "Then, I continued with our team discussion on identifying the main thing, and we did make some progress in that area. Finally, human resources is working on finding some candidates to interview as we try to fill those two open positions on my team.

"The other area that I committed to start working on this week was coaching. Of course, I assumed that coaching for the superstars and middle stars would be positive recognition. I guess my concept was that falling stars were the only ones where I would need to address performance issues.

"However, I have a major issue on my team, and it involves one of my superstars. Here's the deal: Todd has been with our company for four years. He's really good at his job and has a good relationship with all the members of our team. He is dependable, consistent and knowledgeable. But, three weeks ago I discovered that Todd has been drinking on the job. I talked to him about it, and he said that he understood it was wrong, but he was working through some personal issues and was just trying to cope as best he could.

"I told him that I understood, but using alcohol during work hours is against our company policy and our team's code of behavior. So I wrote him a warning letter stating that the next violation would lead to termination.

"Well, last Friday, I saw him drinking again. I happened to be walking by his office around two o'clock and saw him pouring some scotch into his coffee mug. I don't think Todd even saw me. I just kept walking down the hall.

"No one else knows about this situation. If HR knew, they would have already asked me to terminate him. To my knowledge, no one on the team knows about his problem. At the same time, I feel for him — I know he's struggling, and I really want to help him.

"Also, I remembered what you said about raising the top and not lowering the bottom. If I let him go, then I would have three open positions, and I would have lost another one of my superstars, which doesn't help my situation.

"What I think I want to do is to 'forget' what I saw Friday and just watch to see if he does it again. What do you think, Tony?"

My mentor's voice was sympathetic. "I understand where you're coming from, Jeff. I've been there, too. These types of decisions are gut wrenching. And, no, I'm not going to tell you what to do. This must be your decision. However I am going to ask you some questions that may help with your decision-making process.

"First, does Todd understand the company policy and your team's code of behavior about drinking on the job?"

"Yes," I nodded. "In fact, we discussed it in detail in our performance counseling three weeks ago, and he had to sign a document stating he clearly understood the policy as well as the potential consequence."

"Are the policy and your expectations reasonable and fair?" Tony asked.

"Yes, I believe so," I answered.

"So what if one of your falling stars was caught drinking on the job?"

"That's easy," I said. "I would dehire him and move forward. But this is not so easy. Todd is having personal problems, and he's one of my few superstars...and besides, I'd be lowering the top, not raising the bottom!"

Tony paused before his next question. "So, what is the right thing to do?"

"I really don't know," I responded. "I want to be empathetic and help him, but I know he broke the rules. The right thing to do, probably, is let him go. But I would be the one paying the price to do the right thing because then I would have another open position and one less superstar. Frankly, that does not appeal to me."

"Okay, Jeff. Let's think about this from a couple of different perspectives. First, you've mentioned several times that you would be lowering the top if you let Todd go. I don't agree with you. It sounds to me as though you're using that statement to justify not doing the right thing.

"And before you say anything, let me explain. Your job is to raise the top for long-term, sustained success, not for short-term convenience. Short-term results are easy. You can threaten people, pay them more, or just give them what they want, and you can get short-term results.

"Achieving long-term results is much more difficult. It requires establishing a code of behavior that must be followed. It requires providing accurate feedback. It requires delivering the consequences — both positive and negative — based on decisions that employees make. All of these require courage on your part to do the right thing.

"People can be superstars in one area and falling stars in another area. You've categorized Todd as a superstar based on your performance criteria. However it's obvious that he's a falling star based on your code of behavior. So you need to address this issue as though he's a falling star because that's what he is in this area.

"Second, I subscribe to the 'do right rule.' Simply stated, do what is right even when no one is watching! Of course, doing the right thing isn't always easy — in fact sometimes it's real hard — but just remember that doing the right thing is always right.

"Now if you don't have a code of behavior or performance expectations, it's difficult to know what is right. In this case, that's not a problem…at least it doesn't appear to be a problem, based on what you've said.

"Sometimes it's difficult to know what is 'right' when you're in the middle of a crisis like you are right now with this situation. I have found that the best decisions are normally made before you're in a crisis. You can think more clearly and evaluate alternatives better.

"I learned this from a friend of mine who is a pilot. He once told me that every conceivable problem that could happen while he was flying the plane had been simulated, documented, and placed in a contingency manual in the cockpit. That manual documents everything that can go wrong and what actions to take if there's a problem.

"You see, pilots don't make decisions when they're in a crisis — they implement plans that were made before the crisis. For example, if a light is flashing, signaling that there's a hydraulic problem on the aircraft, the pilot opens the manual and finds the procedure for correcting the problem. Then he implements that procedure.

"It would be difficult for a pilot to think of everything he might need to do while he's in a crisis and the plane is losing altitude," he pointed out.

"In business, from time to time we see lights flashing, indicating we have a problem. When that happens, some managers will throw a rug over the light so they can't see it flashing — in other words, they ignore it. Sure, they may feel better, but the company is still losing altitude.

"Other managers may unscrew the bulb...no more annoying light flashing. But when they check the other business gauges, the company is still losing altitude.

"Some may smash the light with a hammer. They may feel better temporarily, but the company is still going down.

"The only way to fix the problem is to go directly to what's causing the light to flash and *fix the problem*. Like the pilot, an action plan should have been decided upon long before the crisis developed.

"If you think about it, you're in the middle of a crisis right now — lights are flashing — and your vision is cloudy. Sure, it's easy to justify going down the least painful path and ignoring the problem instead of doing what is right. But the truth is the problem won't just go away. You have to take action — you have to do what is right and resolve the issue.

"I read where Confucius once said, 'To know what is right and not do it is the worst cowardice.' It sounds as though even Confucius subscribed to the 'do right rule.' But actually living the 'do right rule' is tough because it requires discipline, commitment and courage. Think about it…

"My third question, Jeff, is why do you think you're the only one seeing the problem? Many times the manager is the *last* to know about a problem on the team. What the manager sees is normally a very small part of the whole. It's like an iceberg in the ocean. Above the water you can see the tip, but what lies below is much larger, much more powerful, and usually, much more destructive.

"The closer you are to the situation, the more you can see. Todd's teammates are closer to this 'iceberg' than you are, and I would be surprised if they're not wondering why you are allowing Todd to do what he's doing.

"Fourth, EVERYTHING counts when it comes to your leadership. If you think ignoring the problem doesn't matter, you're wrong — you're always leading, even when you're ignoring a problem. Your team doesn't really care if your company has an ethics department or compliance officer. What matters to your team is what you do. And, everything you do matters because your team is watching…and depending on you to do the right thing.

"Ignoring issues puts your own integrity at risk. And if you lose your integrity, you won't be able to develop or maintain trust, the very basis for relationships. Jeff, I can't say this enough: You must guard your integrity as if it's your most precious leadership possession, because that is what it is. But you are the leader here and the choice is yours.

"Obviously, you have a decision to make. So what are you going to do?"

Tony's message was clear but difficult at the same time. "Okay, I know everything you said is probably correct," I began. "But, it's hard to do what is right when the pressure is on. I'm not looking forward to three open positions, one less superstar — at least in most areas — and facing Todd, knowing he's going through some personal issues. It's tough.

"But, I know I've been fair…and I know he made the choice to put his employment at risk. And I guess you're right — I'm probably not the only person aware of the issue. I think others on the team are watching me and judging me on how I handle this situation.

"I'll go to human resources as soon as I get back to the office, and I'll get their help in working my way though this issue."

I took another deep breath. "Well, Tony. It probably won't surprise you that I already see a place where I need some help from you next week. You mentioned we would discuss hiring at one of these sessions…I think I need to do that pretty fast. Can we do it next week? I've got to make some good hiring decisions — especially now. Wish me luck."

"Good luck this week, Jeff. And we'll plan to cover hiring next week," Tony said. "In the meantime, you'll be fine as you work through this issue. Look at it this way. It's a temporary problem — a temporary problem you have to face. I look forward to hearing about it next week."

DO THE RIGHT THING

✓ Develop your action plan before you get into a crisis.

✓ Guard your integrity like it's your most precious management possession.

The Fifth Monday
Hire Tough

 As I drove up to Tony's house, I could see him at the door.

"Hello, Jeff," he waved. "I'm the one who could hardly wait for you to come this week. In fact, I was tempted to call you several times to find out how your week was going, but I held myself back. So, fill me in."

"Well, it was an interesting week to say the least," I began. "I left here and went straight to Kim in human resources to discuss the Todd issue. She asked me some of the same questions you did, and we decided I didn't have a choice — I had to terminate Todd for drinking on the job.

"So, Kim and I began 'role-playing' the discussion I was about to have with Todd. And, Tony, the role-play helped me feel more prepared and confident. I also asked Kim to witness the termination session. We computed his final pay, got payroll to cut the check, and called him into the conference room.

"Kim's advice to me before the session was that we needed to do everything we could to maintain Todd's self-respect and dignity, while being firm and fair with him.

"When Todd walked into the room, he obviously knew something was up. I asked him to sit down and began talking to him about the drinking problem. He was stunned that I would terminate him for something 'as minor as this.' He also accused me of not having any compassion because he was going through some personal problems. He then went on to say that the team wouldn't survive without him because he was more the leader of the team than I was.

"Thankfully, Kim and I had anticipated and role-played all of his reactions. She said the majority of people who are fired feel the same way: It's someone else's fault, 'management has no heart,' and there are extenuating circumstances. I must admit that she did a great job in preparing me for the meeting. Her last advice before the meeting was to remember that Todd chose to fire himself — we were only implementing his decision. That thought made me feel a little better.

"Anyway, the meeting was 30 extremely long minutes of intense emotions. I really felt badly for Todd, but kept remembering I was only implementing his decision. Finally, he understood we weren't going to debate with him, so he took his check, cleared out his desk and left.

"After taking a few minutes to steady my own emotions, it was then time for my weekly team meeting. Of course, the first thing everyone wanted to know was what happened to Todd. He had left without saying anything, but they saw him clean out his desk. I told them that Todd was no longer with our company and that my number one priority was to fill his position as soon as possible. They asked what happened, and I followed Kim's advice, again, saying I would not go into any details other than we have to work together to take up the slack we all feel without Todd.

"Here was my surprise: I overheard two of my middle stars saying they were relieved they wouldn't have to cover up for Todd's drinking any longer. I don't know if I was the last to discover Todd drinking on the job, but I do know I wasn't the only person aware of the problem. My team was watching and my integrity was being challenged. Tony, you were right again.

"The rest of the meeting went well. We finalized what the main things were for us to accomplish. Here are the three main things we came up with:
1. Treat each person on our team with dignity and respect.
2. Deliver outstanding service to our customers.
3. Provide profits to our company.

"Sound familiar? Almost the same as the main things you told me in our first meeting. I told the team they will be asked, every day, what are the main things. I also told them that if what they were being asked to do by someone else didn't fall into these three areas, they had the right to say no — regardless of who asked.

"So all in all, the week was not too bad. Losing Todd created some logistical issues, but we worked our way through them. I also learned I should have involved Kim in human resources without hesitation. She knows her stuff and wants to help me. In the meantime, she has identified 20 candidates for me to interview for my three open positions. I have interviews scheduled on Wednesday, Thursday and Friday of this week, and I want to fill these positions by the weekend. So I'm anxious to hear what you have to say about hiring."

Now it was Tony's turn to talk. "Great. I'm glad everything worked out with the Todd situation. Jeff, you did the right thing, even though it was tough. I'm proud of you.

"With respect to the hiring, let's start with a question: What is the most valuable asset in your company?"

"That's easy," I said. "People are the most important resource in any company. The people make the company."

"Okay. Now, what is the greatest liability of your company?"

This question was more difficult. "Hmm. I would think that something like product failure would be our greatest liability."

"Well, I don't agree with you on either point," Tony responded.

"I'm not sure I'm right about the greatest liability," I defended, "but I know I'm right about people being the most important asset in our company. How could you argue that? Customers judge our company on the people they deal with. So, people are the most important asset."

"I agree with everything you said — the question was a trick question," Tony admitted. "The most important asset in your company is having the RIGHT PEOPLE on your team. If you have the right people on your team you have a great chance to be successful.

"The greatest liability in your company could be having the WRONG PEOPLE on your team. In fact, there is nothing any competitor can do to hurt your team as much as having the wrong person on the team.

"The most important thing you do as a leader is to hire the right people. You cannot have a strong and effective team with weak and ineffective people.

"Jeff, you have a great opportunity right now. With three open positions, you can make a big difference in the make-up of your team. You can add some diversity, generate new ideas, and add some energy and spark by picking the right people to join your team.

"You said that you wanted to hire these three people by the weekend," he continued. "I don't think that is reasonable. Your job is to hire tough — make it a privilege for someone to earn his or her way on your team. If you hire tough, it will be a whole lot easier to manage the RIGHT PEOPLE.

"The decision you have to make is to hire tough and manage easy, or hire easy and manage tough. I can assure you that the best thing to do is to take your time on the front end so that you can enjoy having the RIGHT PEOPLE on your team.

"When you begin the process of interviewing and hiring, understand up front that you are probably not a great interviewer. Don't take that personally — it's not a poor reflection on you. It's just that you don't use your interviewing skills very often. If you don't use the skills very often, you need a good system to help you make the best decision. I'm sure that Kim in HR will provide you with an interviewing track to follow. And you may even want to ask her to participate in the hiring process with you.

"The first mistake some people make in interviewing is lack of preparation. You shouldn't begin preparing for the interview when the candidate is in the lobby. Is that the way you want to treat some-one who may become your most valuable asset? Every question should be prepared in advance so you spend your time listening and evaluating instead of trying to figure out what question you want to ask next.

"Another problem with interviewing is you're always emotionally involved. The open position is taking time and energy away from you, so you want to fill the job fast. Fight those emotions. You will be far better off by taking your time and getting the right person. I suggest you ask Kim or someone in HR to help — they're not faced with the same emotions you have about these openings.

"The Three Rules of Three in hiring are: interview at least three qualified candidates for every position; interview the candidates three times; and have three people evaluate the candidates. I know that sounds like a long process, but remember — your job is to hire tough.

"Kim has already provided you with 20 qualified candidates for the three positions. That's good. You have more choices. After the initial interviews, narrow the field down to your best nine candidates. I would schedule interviews with those nine candidates at times that are different than their original interview time. In other words, if your initial interview was in the morning with one person, interview them the next time in the afternoon or evening. You'll be working with them all day, so why not see what they're like at different times of the day?

"Since you and Kim are involved in the process, you may want to allow one of your superstars to be involved as well. The superstar may be able to give you some insight on how the candidate would fit with your current team.

"If there is any question whether a person is qualified or not, pass on them and keep searching for the right person. Never lower your standards just to fill a position! You'll pay for it later.

"I see that our time is up for today. So tell me, what are you going to do differently during this coming week?"

"Well, first I'm going to slow down the hiring process and do it right. My goal is to hire tough and make it an honor for someone to be on our team. Next, I'm going to involve Kim and one of my superstars in the process — and I will follow the Three Rules of Three so that I have enough information to make a great decision.

"I know this is the most important decision I'll make, and I'm going to do my very best to make a great decision," I finished, thinking of how much information Tony had shared that I could use right away.

"You're a good student, Jeff, and I can feel your enthusiasm about your opportunity to bring some new people to your team. Hire tough!"

"See you next week!"

HIRE TOUGH

✓ The most important asset in your company is having the RIGHT PEOPLE on your team.

✓ Never lower your standards just to fill a position! You will pay for it later.

The Sixth Monday
Do Less or Work Faster

By this time, I so looked forward to my Monday Mornings with Tony, that I was getting up much earlier...and feeling much better about so many aspects of what had once been such a disaster area, both at work and at home.

I pulled into Tony's driveway well before our meeting time, but when I rang the bell, Tony appeared, as charming as always. "Good morning, Jeff," he said. "How are things going? Did you make any progress filling your open positions?"

"Yes, I made some real progress, Tony. Kim and I interviewed all 20 candidates for the three open positions. It was pretty taxing, but Kim provided me with a good process to follow, and we have narrowed the 20 down to nine possible candidates. The final round of interviews are scheduled for Wednesday, Thursday, and Friday this week. By our next meeting I should have offered the jobs to the three best candidates.

"And I'll tell you — after our conversation last week, I'm taking the hiring process much more seriously," I confessed.

"But this hiring process has been so time consuming, I've hardly done anything else. And that's another issue I wanted your insights on — how do I get everything done?

"Even though I feel I've made a lot of progress during our sessions, it seems my time continues to be consumed by things outside my control. It's frustrating because I want to spend more time with my team...and my family."

"Jeff, you sound the same as you did in our first meeting: 'Woe is me...I have no control over my time.' Well it sounds to me like you may be blaming your personal time management problem on things outside your control. Let me ask you this: Who can spend your time but you?"

"Aren't you being a little harsh?" I countered, defensively. "I simply said I seem to be consumed by things I feel I don't have much control over, and so I'm not able to do the important things I need — and want — to do."

"Sorry if I came across harshly," Tony apologized. "I'm trying to make a point: Your time is your responsibility. If you aren't able to do the important things, only you can solve that problem. Your team is depending on you to be there for them, and that includes solving your personal problems.

"One of the major sources of stress, anxiety, and unhappiness comes from feeling like your life is out of control. You need to figure out ways to take control of your time so that you can take control of your life.

"Of course, there are some things we can't change about the way we spend our time. We have to wait in lines, at red lights, for elevators, and things like that. There's not much we can do about those things. However there is a lot we can do about situations at work.

"Jeff, I've studied time management for years — in fact it's one of my favorite pastimes — and I've discovered that there are no magic bullets when it comes to time management. I've never found anyone who had two or three hours a day they could save by doing one thing better. But, I have seen many people find an hour or two a day they could use better by doing a few things differently.

"If you want to make better use of your time, you need to be looking for the small increments of time...a minute here, five minutes there, etc. Add them all up and you'll create more time for you to use.

"I have also found that the job seldom overworks the person, but people often overwork themselves by making bad time management decisions. The bottom line is that most people can't solve their time problem by working harder. Doing the wrong thing harder doesn't help. What we need to do is to find ways to shorten tasks, eliminate some steps, combine some tasks, and work easier while getting things done.

"There's a myth out there no one seems to recognize, and it's this: No one can save time...we all have the same amount, and we can't carry any time over to the next day. So since we can't save time, we have to make better decisions on how we spend our time.

"I only know of two ways to spend time better. You can do less or you can do things faster. Those are our only choices. Of course there are some things we could eliminate and just say no to. But for today's session, let's say that the only option we have is to work faster. So how can you work faster? That's the question we need to address.

"The first thing you need to figure out is where your time is currently going. If you want to make improvements, you've got to know what to improve. To find the answer, I suggest you track your time for two weeks so you can make some educated decisions about what to improve.

"You will find that your time is taken by the things we do and how we do things. Follow me on this: We spend our time doing the main things or doing the wrong things...and we spend our time doing things right or doing things wrong.

"For example, here's a chart showing the four choices of how we can spend our time in a meeting:

How We Do the Things We Do		
	Main Things Right Example: Run a productive and necessary meeting.	**Main Things Wrong** Example: Waste two hours during an important meeting.
	Wrong Things Right Example: Facilitate a great meeting that was not necessary.	**Wrong Things Wrong** Example: Waste everyone's time at an unnecessary meeting.

(left axis label: **The Things We Do**)

"Everything we do can be categorized into one of those four choices. If you keep track for two weeks, you'll know what you can do to make some better decisions. You've already identified the main things in your department. Now, classify your activities — are you doing those main things and how well are you doing them?

"Most executives have three areas where they can make changes that will lead to major time improvements: prioritizing/organizing, inter-ruptions, and meetings.

"While preparing for our session, I gathered some of the best tips I've found about managing my time in each of those areas. Let's talk about *prioritizing and organizing* first.

"You've probably heard of the Pareto Principle that states that 80% of your results will come from 20% of your activities. An Italian economist named Alfredo Pareto discovered the principle in the 1800's when he observed that 20% of the people in Italy controlled 80% of the wealth. Then he began looking around and discovered that the 80/20 rule applied to many things. And the Pareto Principle definitely applies to time management. It's your responsi-bility to yourself and your team to know where your highest payoff activities are and eliminate as many as you can of the ones that yield few results.

"Every time management guru will tell you to **touch paper only once.** The key to paper management is to keep the paper moving: Throw it away, act upon it, or put it into your reading pile. It may not be reasonable to only touch paper once in every situation, but remember — shuffling and reshuffling paper from pile to pile with no evaluation or action is wasting your time.

"One of the most important personal tips for me is to **set aside some uninterrupted planning time every day.** It was difficult for me to discipline myself to do this, but I found that spending 20 uninter-rupted minutes planning would yield the same results as 60 minutes of interrupted time. If you can't set aside 20 minutes, set aside 10. That's still a great return on your time investment.

"**Conduct an audit on every report that hits your in-box.** Is the report really necessary? If not, eliminate it. If you only need a line item off a report, ask the originator of the report to eliminate the report and send you the line item.

"**Clean your desk.** I think you should always be able to see the majority of the top of your desk. Don't fool yourself into thinking that a cluttered desk makes you look important. A cluttered desk makes you look disorganized and contributes to the shuffling and re-shuffling game.

"**Control your email deliveries.** You don't go to your mailbox every 30 minutes, do you? I receive a lot of emails every day — I could be at my computer all day just responding to emails. Instead, I work my email deliveries into my personal schedule so that emails don't control my day.

"**Batch activities — do like activities together — so that you're not starting and stopping all the time.** Do all your voice mails at once. Return all phone calls at one time. Write memos or letters at one sitting. Eliminate as many transitions from one activity to another as possible.

"Here's a simple one that can give you ten, maybe fifteen minutes every day. **Go to lunch at 11 or 1.** Why everyone decides to go to lunch at noon is a mystery to me. They wait on the elevator, wait in line at the deli, wait in line to get back on the elevator, and then complain about not having enough time for lunch.

"Now let's talk about another key area of time management — *interruptions.*

"Most people don't know who is interrupting them or why they're being interrupted. **Keep track of who is interrupting you and why they're interrupting you.** Then you can make some informed decisions about how you're going to address the problem.

"I have found that **even if you can't eliminate the interruption — you can keep it short.** A general rule is this: The length of the interruption is in direct proportion to the comfort level of the interrupter. Don't let the interrupter sit down and get comfortable in your office. When someone comes into your office, stand up. You can take care of business standing up more quickly than — and just as well as — sitting down.

"Your furniture can even invite interruptions and steal some time from you. I suggest you **arrange your furniture so that your desk doesn't face the flow of traffic.** If you're looking at every person who walks down the hall, you'll be wasting a lot of time.

"**Schedule one-on-one sessions with your staff and boss** so that you can get as much as possible accomplished at one time. Gather everything you need to talk about and take care of it at one sitting rather than interrupting each other the minute something comes up.

"You may want to **ask your team: 'What do I do that wastes your time and hinders your performance?'** Some of their suggestions may surprise you and could save you and your team valuable time.

"Finally, let's talk about one of the biggest time wasters I know of — *meetings.*

"Jeff, I've been to a gazillion meetings in my day and have found that

— if everyone is prepared, on-time and focused — most meetings can be accomplished in half the time the meeting is currently taking. The average person wastes about 250 hours per year in unproductive meetings. That's a lot of time and money being wasted! **Make your meetings productive but short.**

"Don't fall into the 'perpetually scheduled meeting' syndrome where you're having meetings just because meetings are regularly scheduled. Make sure every meeting is absolutely necessary. Routine meetings are not a good investment unless they fulfill, or move forward, your objectives.

"Always begin a meeting by covering the most important items first. That way you ensure that you cover what you need to accomplish, and you're not rushing through the main things.

"When people show up late, don't recap what you've covered. When you recap, you're rewarding the tardy person and punishing the people who were on time.

"Probably the simplest tip that pays the biggest dividend in meeting management is to **start and end your meetings on time.** It's disrespectful and a bad investment to start a meeting later than scheduled. You waste 30 minutes of productivity by beginning a meeting with 10 people three minutes late. Think about that.

"These are just a few ideas to help you make better use of your time. There are many more. I suggest you invest some time in reading a book on time management and look for several other areas where you can find a few extra minutes.

"Speaking of time, our time is about up for this week," said Tony, following his own counsel. "So, what are you going to do differently next week?"

"Well, I'm going to finish the hiring process," I replied. "That's the main thing of all main things this week. While you were talking, I was doing a self-check on the meetings I facilitate, and I know I can do a better job creating some additional time for my team and myself. I'm also going to track who interrupts me and the number of times that I interrupt others. I may be guilty of being the #1 interrupter to my team members. And I'm going to buy a book on time management and search for other ideas to help me gain control of my time and my life."

"Great, Jeff!" Tony's enthusiastic response energized my own resolve. "Try out some of those ideas. I know you'll find some more time for yourself and your family."

"See you next week!"

DO LESS/WORK FASTER

✓ Your time is your responsibility. Take control of your time so you can take control of your life.

✓ Look for small increments of time by prioritizing, limiting interruptions, and effectively managing meetings.

The Seventh Monday
Buckets and Dippers

 I arrived at Tony's promptly at 8:30 a.m. He greeted me at the door.

"Jeff, how are you today and how was your week?" he said, guiding me into the library. "Did you make any progress filling your open positions? And how about your time management? Did you find any places where you could spend your time better? And of course, I want to hear how the team is doing."

I had spent the weekend looking forward to our Monday morning conversation. "Last week was a much better week. Kim and I completed the interviewing and made job offers to the best three candidates," I said.

"Two of them accepted and start in a couple of weeks. One person turned us down and decided to stay at his current company. I was going to offer the job to our next best candidate, but Mark (one of my superstars who helped interview) said the next best candidate didn't fit well with our current team. He suggested we keep looking for a more qualified candidate.

"Since you said to hire tough and never lower my standards, I asked Kim to begin the process of finding the right person for our last open position. And yes, I'm really excited about the two new team members.

"I also tried several of your time management tips. I kept a log of where I was spending my time and discovered I was spending a lot of time on things that weren't important. I also found one particular person in our office interrupted me at least six times a day. I showed her my log of how many times we were talking to each other in a day, and she couldn't believe she called me that often.

"So, we made a deal to talk at 10 a.m. and 3 p.m. only. I guess you would call that 'batching.'

"I also cut our weekly team meeting time in half. We normally allow an hour for our meeting, and we seem to go the full hour whether we need to or not. This week, I said we needed to cover everything faster and be finished in 30 minutes. Well, you know what? We did it. We started with our most important items and finished them all. That gave everyone on the team an extra 30 minutes that day, which we used for uninterrupted planning.

"We wanted to test your theory that we could accomplish in 30 minutes of uninterrupted time what would normally take us 90 minutes to do while being interrupted. The theory worked in reality! Some of my cynical troops weren't sure that we accomplished in 30 minutes what normally took us 90, but everybody agreed that we at least doubled our productivity in those 30 minutes. That's a good deal.

"See, Tony. I was listening to you, and those were some great ideas. I do feel like I'm more in control of my time now, but I still have a way to go. I also bought a book on time management to read when I find the time."

"So now you're a comedian?" Tony chuckled. "You did make some great choices last week. It sounds as though the new people have the talent and desire to be on your team. And you made some better choices in how you spent your time. Good job!

"Now, if I were you, I would approach Chad and Jeni about your open position. You already know they're superstars and will fit in with your team. You may have to swallow your pride when you ask them to come back, but I think it's a good idea.

"Look in your spiral notebook at the notes you made when you talked to Chad and Jeni. They mentioned three things that they expected from you. What were they?"

"Well, let's see," I said, leafing back to the front of the book. "They said they needed me to hire good people, coach every member of the team to become better, and dehire the people who aren't carrying their share of the load. Is that what you were asking?"

"Yes," Tony said. "And how have 'we' done in those three areas?"

"I think I've made great progress in hiring other good people to be on the team," I answered. "Tony, you've taught me well and I'm now hiring tough. Kim also was a great support throughout the process, and I really feel good about the two new people who are coming on board.

"As far as coaching every team member to become better, I think I've made a little progress. I'm paying more attention to the superstars and middle stars. But I really haven't focused very much on coaching my good performers.

"Of course, I had to dehire Todd. Amazingly, I thought he was a superstar until I found out others on the team were covering for him. I guess that just proves I was spending too much time in management land.

"Before I begin more dehiring, I need to better define my expectations and ensure that the proper training and tools are in place. Through this entire process, I discovered that the performance reviews I've been giving don't accurately reflect performance. So, I have a lot of work to do in the dehiring area."

"Well, Jeff, it sounds as though you're at least making progress in addressing the three things Chad and Jeni suggested. Great job," my mentor said encouragingly.

"For the remainder of our time today, let's focus on how you can coach every member of the team to become better. Now, I'm not talking about performance improvement sessions. I'm talking about recognition of, and communication to, everyone on the team.

"A few weeks ago we talked about a place called 'management land' and how sometimes we get caught up in the things happening in management land while we overlook important things on the team. Here are two facts you should never forget, regardless of your title or position:

1. "Your scorecard as a leader is the result of your team. You are needed; you are important. But you get paid for what your subordinates do, not necessarily what you do.

2. "You need your team more than your team needs you.

Don't get me wrong — you need each other, but cumulatively, the 17 people on your team accomplish much more than you do.

"To make my point, answer a couple of questions. First, what percentage of the work that needs to be done is getting done while you're here with me this morning?" As always, Tony's questions went right to the heart of the issue.

"I think they're probably getting about 95 percent of the work accomplished, even while I'm not there," I admitted.

"Okay, I would agree — ninety-five percent is probably an accurate number. Some of your people may say 105 percent — they get more done while you're away — maybe so, but let's go with your 95 percent.

"Now, let's suppose your 17 people were here with me, and you were the only one left at the office. What percentage of the work would be getting done then?" he asked.

"Not much! I would probably get about 10 percent of the work done," I responded as honestly as I could.

"So your team is accomplishing 95 percent, and you can only accomplish 10 percent? Then who needs who the most? Obviously you need each other, but never forget that your job is to help each team member become better at the job they've chosen. They have entrusted a portion of their life to you, and it's your job to help them grow, personally and professionally. So you need to do everything you can to help them become the very best!

"Follow me on this analogy: Every person has a bucket of motivation. That bucket can be filled to overflowing, or it can be empty and desperately need filling. Sometimes the buckets have leaks…and those buckets lose motivation as fast as you can try to motivate.

"Every person also has a dipper. In fact some people have these great big, long dippers that they enjoy putting into other people's buckets. Their dippers represent cynicism, negativism, confusion, stress, doubt, fear, anxiety, and any other thing that can drain someone's desire and motivation.

"As a leader, your job is to keep everyone's bucket filled. You are the Chief Bucket-Filler, and the best way to fill buckets is with excellent communication. In fact, there are four things you have to do if you're going to keep your team members' motivation buckets full.

"**First, a full bucket requires knowing what are the main things that are important to doing a good job.** We talked about this before, and you and your team have now identified the main things. But if people don't know what the main thing is, their motivation bucket will leak like a bucket full of shotgun holes. A leader with focus and direction fills buckets. A leader who creates confusion and inconsistency has a dipper that drains people's buckets.

"**Second, to keep buckets filled, you need to provide the bucket holders with feedback on how they're doing.** You may think a performance appraisal will keep a bucket full, but it won't. Performance appraisals may fill a bucket for a short period of time, but the bucket will have leaks in it after a few days. Don't get me wrong — performance reviews are important and necessary to document performance, but they don't provide long-term motivation.

"People need to know how they're doing all the time, not just at performance review time. But here's a warning: you can have great intentions to fill buckets and yet be draining buckets if you don't follow the rules of effective feedback.

"*Be sincere.* If you're not sincere about your feedback, people will see through you like a crystal glass. Insincere feedback is a great big dipper into someone's bucket.

"*To fill buckets, your feedback has to be specific.* If you're not specific with your praise, the bucket will not fill up. Why? Because the bucket holder will tip over the bucket while scratching his or her head, wondering what you're talking about.

"*Feedback must be timely.* The more time you wait to fill the bucket, the more other people's dippers will get into the bucket. Then you'll have to work twice as hard to fill it back up.

"*Feedback must be aligned with the receiver's value system.* Don't try to fill someone's bucket with something that's important to you but not to them. Bucket filling is in the eye of the bucket holder, not the bucket filler.

"**The third thing you have to do to keep your team members' buckets filled is to let them know you care about them and the job they do.** There are a gazillion ways to show you care and fill your team's buckets. Of course, the paycheck they get fills their buckets, but the buckets will dry up if you only bucket-fill on days that you hand them a paycheck. Find those bucket fillers that work best with your team, and then use them to fill their buckets often.

"Here are a dozen ways to show your team members you care about them — they seem to work well for other bucket fillers I know:

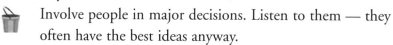 Involve people in major decisions. Listen to them — they often have the best ideas anyway.

Memorize facts about the bucket holder and their family. People enjoy sharing what's happening in their families. Let them fill their own buckets while you listen.

Make coffee for your team. Making coffee is a pretty simple act that people appreciate — it's an easy bucket filler.

Send thank you notes to team members at home. People normally only get bills and junk mail at home. A positive note of recognition goes a long way to filling a bucket.

Send bucket holders a Thanksgiving card. Your success is dependent on them — who else at work would you be more thankful for?

Ask your superstars — if they're interested — to become mentors for middle stars or falling stars. This is a win/win — everyone's buckets get filled.

Keep a camera close by to record significant bucket-filling events.

Plant a tree on company property in honor of your team.

Create a library of books, tapes, and magazines, and keep it current and well stocked so team members can fill their own buckets.

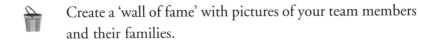

Create a 'wall of fame' with pictures of your team members and their families.

Follow the platinum bucket-filling rule: Treat people the way *they* wish to be treated.

Spend time with all your team members. Sometimes simply being around and showing that you care about them will automatically fill their buckets.

"The fourth and final bucket-filling requirement is for the team to know how well it's doing as a team. Everyone wants to be on a winning team. Make sure team members consistently know whether the team is accomplishing its objectives or not.

"If you will fulfill the four bucket-filling requirements — know the main things, give feedback on performance, provide recognition for doing a good job, and communicate the team score — your team members will be asking you what they can do to help fill your bucket. That's the way it works. The more buckets you fill, the more your bucket is filled."

Tony glanced at his watch. "Well once again, our time is up. So, what are you going to do before next week?"

"Several things. First, I'm going to call Jeni and Chad to see if they're interested in returning to the team. I'm going to share with them the changes I'm making, and will continue to make, to become a better leader.

"I really like your bucket-filling analogy. In fact, I'm going to share it with my team. If we will keep our dippers out of each other's buckets, I think we can all be more motivated, productive and happy. I may even give them a bucket and dipper to drive home the analogy and have some fun," I said.

"Great, Jeff, and good luck with Jeni and Chad. I hope that works out well for you. Next week is our last session. We'll spend our time talking about you and what you can do to accomplish your personal goals. I look forward to seeing you then."

FILL LOTS OF BUCKETS

✓ 4 Ways to fill buckets:
1. Know the main things
2. Give feedback on performance
3. Provide recognition
4. Communicate the team score

✓ The more buckets you fill, the more your bucket is filled.

The Eighth Week
Enter the Learning Zone

"Welcome, Jeff. It's your graduation day," beamed Tony as we shook hands and headed for his library. "The last time I went to your graduation, I told you the learning was just beginning. The same thing applies now, even after all the years of experience you have. Truth be known, I've probably learned more in our sessions than you have. Thank you for allowing me to share with you."

"Wait! Don't thank me," I protested. "You gave your time and knowledge to me!"

I could tell Tony was uneasy with my praise.

"Well, enough of the boola-boola," he said. "What happened last week at work?"

"Well, the best news is Jeni is coming back to the company. I explained the changes I was making in how I lead the team. Then, I think she called several of her friends to see if I was really doing what I had outlined in our conversation — and to find out if it was making a difference. She called on Wednesday, saying she really wanted to come back to the team. She starts in two weeks. That's a good deal.

"The new hires are doing great. They're full of enthusiasm, and it's rubbing off on the rest of the team…including me. It was worth the time and effort to hire tough and get the right people on board.

"I shared your analogy of the bucket and the dipper with the team. Then we brainstormed some of our own rules for bucket-filling and what to do when someone gets their dipper in your bucket. Not only was it a fun exercise, it definitely made a point. A couple of times last week I heard people say, 'Get your dipper out of my bucket!' when a negative or cynical comment was made.

"That's about it. Things are going pretty smoothly now that we have focus."

"That's good news, Jeff. Remember I told you this last session would be all about you?" Tony's tone was back to its serious pitch. "We've spent seven sessions talking about your team, your leadership style, and how to get results from others.

"Now let's focus on what you can do to achieve the goals you have for yourself.

"First, I want to commend you. It took courage for you to call me several weeks ago. You might not have called unless you were at a point where you had nothing to lose, but you still had the courage to call. I understand that feeling of being at the end of your rope. I've been there before and made a similar call, out of the blue, to an old friend. If you hadn't had the courage to make the call, most likely nothing would have changed except you'd probably be even more frustrated. Anyway, I'm glad you called.

"Did you see the movie *Ground Hog Day* — the one where Bill Murray lives the same day over and over again?"

"Yes, pretty funny movie," I said.

"Well, that's the way many people live their lives," Tony explained. "They wake up and do the same things over and over and over — because that's where they're comfortable — until it's time to retire.

"Jeff, you have too much potential to be living *Ground Hog Day* over and over.

"A forceful enemy to your potential is your comfort zone. When you first came to my home eight weeks ago, without knowing it, you described what it was like to be in the comfort zone. And then things changed at work, and the comfort zone was no longer comfortable. You didn't know what to do or where to go.

"For you to be the very best, you cannot allow yourself to become complacent in your comfort zone. You need to be reaching for improvement. To fulfill your potential, you need to move out of your comfort zone and into 'the learning zone.'

"Let me explain. There are three rooms in the learning zone. The first room is the reading room. Look around this library — there are more than a thousand books in here. More than half of those books are about management and leadership. Executives call me to help them solve business problems. I've never 'made up' a solution. None of their problems are unique. The value I offer is the wisdom of all the people who have written these books.

"You learn more by reading more. I'm living proof that the more you learn, the more you earn.

"Did you know most people don't read one non-fiction book in a year? Not one. You'd think books must be scarce or expensive. But there is an abundance of books at every public library, waiting for people to simply walk in and check them out — at no charge — free!

"Now let's suppose you decided to read one book a month on management or leadership. Most books are between 12 and 20 chapters, so you'd be reading about half a chapter a day, which would take you about 10 minutes. During the next year, you'd have read 12 books. Do you think you'd know more about management and leadership if you read 12 books a year on the subject?"

This was a rare no-brainer question for our Monday mornings. "Of course," I said.

"When the next job opening at a higher position in the company comes up, would you be better prepared to assume that role?"

"Of course!"

"See, Jeff, the question is NOT do you have the time or money. The question is do you have the DISCIPLINE to set aside time every day to read. In your case, you probably won't retire for at least 15 years. In 15 years, you could read 180 books just by reading half a chapter a day. Make it a priority to read, and your knowledge will likely make you the obvious choice for the next promotion.

"The second room in the learning zone is the listening room. Did you know that the principal reasons executives fail are arrogance, out-of-control egos, and insensitivity?

"They forget to take the time to listen to their people. Soon they become insensitive to the needs and desires of the individuals on the team. Arrogance, out-of-control egos, and insensitivity are part of the management land trap. Don't allow yourself to fall into that trap — listen to your people!

"A few other comments about listening. First, you tend to listen better when you attend outside seminars and conferences. Any time you gather new information, you can make better decisions.

"Second, you can also learn to listen better by making better use of your time while you're in your car. The average person spends over 500 hours per year in their car. That's a lot of time. Maybe if you spent some of that time listening to a motivational or inspirational audiotape, it would have a greater influence on you than listening to talk radio or music. It's just a thought…

"The third room in the learning zone is the giving room. I strongly feel you cannot succeed without giving back," Tony continued. "There are reasons why hearses don't have luggage racks! Your legacy will be what you leave others. When we started these sessions, one of the requirements was that you would have to teach others what I was teaching you. My purpose in making that a requirement was so you would become more accountable. The more you teach, the more accountable you become to what you're teaching. Teaching is good for you!

"I realize it's easy to agree we need to become life-long learners. But the facts are that nothing is going to change unless you set specific goals for improvement.

"You may have heard the story of people who went to the airport to wait for their ship to come in. The only problem is, ships don't go to airports! If you want your ship to come in, you've got to go where the ships are. In personal improvement, the ships are in goals — specific, measurable, and obtainable goals.

"I've found that goals can become the strongest force for self-motivation — they are your track to run your course. Yet less than five percent of all people set specific goals, and fewer than five percent will write their goals down on paper.

"If goals are so important, why don't more people set them?" Tony asked, rhetorically. "I think there are four main reasons why people fail to set goals. First, people fail to set goals because they don't know the importance of goal setting. Every great accomplishment I know about has begun with a goal written down on a sheet of paper. Achieving the goal is automatic. Setting the goal is the issue.

"Second, most people don't know how to set goals. After each session, I asked you to write down what actions you were going to take the next week. I did that because writing clarifies the goal and commits you to it.

"Third, sometimes people don't set goals because they're afraid of failure. If you have no goals, you're not risking failure. I think we should do the opposite — fail faster and more often. Failure is a prelude to success. To become more successful, we have to fail more often...but don't take this to an extreme. I'm talking about setting goals that will help us become more successful even if we fail to accomplish the goal.

"Fourth, goals require people to leave their comfort zone. That can be scary for many people because it often involves having to learn new skills.

"Nothing would please me more than to watch you become a fantastic goal setter and goal achiever. You can become a leader who has balance in your life. You can become a great role model for others to follow. But over the years, I've learned that most people don't want to follow someone who loses their health or their family because they work all the time. People want to follow people who are balanced in all areas, not just work.

"My final thought for you is this: Stay positive! Of course you will become discouraged again somewhere along the way. Just don't give up.

"The world is not for Pollyannas. Bad things happen to even the best people. You know how much I enjoy golf. Well, I think golf is a great teacher of life's lessons as well as leadership lessons. And, I've learned that in every round of golf, three bad things are going to happen that are not deserved.

"You may hit the ball in the middle of the fairway only to discover the ball in an old divot. Or, you hit the perfect shot right before the wind gusts, and your shot lands just short, buried in the bunker. Or perhaps your perfect putt moves off course because someone didn't take time to fix their ball mark.

"Similar unfair things happen in business. The question is not, 'Are unfair things going to happen?' The question is, 'How are you going to react to whatever happens?'

"I have one last story for you:

"I once knew an older woman who I would consider one of the wisest and most positive persons I've ever known. She didn't have much money or formal education, nor did she work outside the home. Yet she had earned a PhD in common sense and wisdom.

"One of the nuggets of wisdom from this old friend that I will always remember is how to face problems and be positive, no matter the situation.

"She loved to tell the story of how everyone could go to a field — about the size of a football field — and line up around the perimeter. While standing on the edge of the field, each person is given the opportunity to throw their problems into the middle of the field. Once all the problems have been thrown in, you have your choice of which ones to pick up and take home. Most people will probably pick up their own problems and go back home, realizing that they really didn't have it that bad after all.

"You know, I think she's right on the money with her story! So much of life is about attitude and how we handle what life throws our way. Life is good — even when a situation appears to be the worst. Stay positive and help make another's life better!

"So, Jeff, we are about out of time. And, for the last time, I'll ask my question: What are you going to do differently?"

"Well, Tony, I think you saved your best story for last, and I think your friend is probably right.

"I suspected you would ask me what I would do differently one more time, so I came prepared. I've reviewed my notes from all the previous sessions, and here are my commitments:

Jeff's Leadership Commitments

✓ I am responsible for my actions and my team's performance, no matter what the circumstances.

✓ I keep the main thing the main thing.

✓ I have a positive relationship with my boss.

✓ I escape from management land and stay in tune with my people.

✓ I recognize and reward superstar activity.

✓ I address problems in a pro-active manner.

✓ I do what's right even when no one is watching.

✓ I realize that everything I do counts toward my leadership score.

✓ I hire tough.

✓ I am an excellent time manager.

✓ I fill other's buckets.

"And after this week's session, I'm going to add two more:
- ✓ I live in the learning zone.
- ✓ I am a positive role model for others."

"Wonderful, Jeff! My, you have come a long way in the past eight weeks," Tony said, standing and shaking my hand.

"Before I leave, I have something for you in my car," I said. "I'll be right back."

"Here, Tony. This is for you," I said, handing him a gift-wrapped box.

Tony opened the present — a big brass bucket with Tony's initials engraved on the front. It was filled to overflowing with 30 or so small gifts.

"At the risk of sounding corny, this gift represents what you have done for me the past eight weeks," I explained, a lump beginning in my throat. "You filled my bucket with your gifts of insight and wisdom.

"So my question to you is, 'When can we meet again?'"

"Well, remember — when we began our sessions you committed to teach others what I would be teaching you. Do that and then we'll get together. Thank you for the bucket and gifts, Jeff. I am honored that you called me and allowed me to work with you."

I took a deep breath as I walked outside and turned to wave. "So long, Tony. See you soon!"

LIVE IN THE
LEARNING ZONE

✓ Get out of the comfort zone

✓ Read 10 minutes a day

✓ Listen to people

✓ Give back

✓ Set goals

✓ Stay positive

Epilogue

Present day...

My eight Monday Mornings with Tony served as the turning point in my career. His gentle wisdom has guided my actions and my path during the past two years.

Six months ago, I was promoted and Jeni, who left our company and then came back, took over my old position.

Most people don't have — and will never have — the luxury of a mentor like Tony. My desire is that you will be able to learn from him and pass on this knowledge to others.

Now I can make my call to Tony to set up our next meeting...

Wisdom from Tony
A Collection of Quotations

*"When it comes to leading people,
there is no problem that is unique to you."*

Page 19

*"Even though your responsibilities increase
when you become a manager, you lose some of the rights
or freedoms you may have enjoyed in the past."*

Page 21

*"A real leader spends his time fixing the problem
instead of finding who to blame."*

Page 22

*"When you write things down, you commit to doing them.
If you simply tell me what you want to do,
there is really no commitment to getting it done."*

Page 23

*"When you depend on another's perceptions
to match your expectations,
you're setting yourself up for disappointment."*
Page 29

❖

"People quit people before they quit companies."
Page 29

❖

*"Take the time to manage your boss
the same way you manage your subordinates."*
Page 31

❖

*"One of the 'main things' for a leader
is to eliminate confusion."*
Page 36

❖

*"You have to escape from management land
and get in touch with your people."*
Page 37

*"Your job is not to lower the bottom
by adjusting for and acommodating
the lowest performing employees. You should be
raising the top by recognizing
and rewarding superstar behaviors!"*
Page 40

*"Doing the right thing isn't always easy —
in fact sometimes it's real hard — but just remember
that doing the right thing is always right."*
Page 47

*"Everything you do matters
because your team is watching… and depending
on you to do the right thing."*
Page 49

*"Guard your integrity
as if it's your most precious leadership possession,
because that is what it is."*
Page 50

"The most important thing you do as a leader is to hire the right people."
Page 57

❖

"Never lower your standards just to fill a position. You will pay for it later."
Page 59

❖

"One of the major sources of stress, anxiety, and unhappiness comes from feeling like your life is out of control."
Page 62

❖

"If you want to make better use of your time, you need to be looking for the small increments of time… a minute here, five minutes there, etc."
Page 63

❖

*"You are the Chief Bucket-Filler,
and the best way to fill buckets
is with excellent communication."*
Page 76

❖

*"For you to be the very best, you cannot allow yourself
to become complacent in your comfort zone.
You need to be reaching for improvement."*
Page 85

❖

*"So much of life is about attitude and how we handle
what life throws our way. Life is good —
even when a situation appears to be the worst."*
Page 90

The CornerStone Principles of Leadership

Values Principles

The Principle of Integrity – Results improve in proportion to the level of trust earned by the leader.

The Principle of Responsibility – Results improve when leaders and their followers are held accountable for their actions.

The Principle of Commitment – Results improve to the extent that the leader hires and develops talented people.

The Principle of Vision – Results improve when leaders establish a crystal-clear vision with a convincing reason to embrace the vision.

Synergy Principles

The Principle of Communication – Results improve when followers understand their role and are rewarded for their accomplishments.

The Principle of Conflict Resolution – Results improve when the leader removes obstacles inhibiting followers.

The Principle of Optimism – Results improve in proportion to the self-esteem and attitude of the leader.

The Principle of Change Management – Results improve to the extent the leader embraces change and makes change positive.

The CornerStone Principles of Leadership
(continued)

Investment Principles

The Principle of Empowerment – Results improve as followers are allowed to accept responsibility for their actions.

The Principle of Courage – Results improve in proportion to the leader's ability to confront issues affecting his followers.

The Principle of Example – Results improve when the leader is a positive role model.

The Principle of Preparation – Results improve to the extent that leaders develop themselves and their followers.

About the Author

David Cottrell, President and CEO of CornerStone Leadership Institute, is an internationally-known leadership consultant, educator, and speaker. His business experience includes senior management positions with Xerox and FedEx. He also led the successful turn-around of a chapter eleven company before founding CornerStone.

David's 25-plus years of professional experience are reflected in eleven highly acclaimed books and his reputation as a premier public speaker. David has been a featured expert on public television and has presented his leadership message to over 25,000 managers worldwide.

Keynotes & Seminars with David Cottrell

David Cottrell is a thought provoking and electrifying professional speaker. His powerful wisdom and insights on leadership and customer service have made him a highly sought after keynote speaker and seminar leader.

David Cottrell's seminars are customized to reinforce your company mission, vision, and values. The content is practical for team leaders, managers, supervisors and sales professionals.

A partial list of recent clients includes:

AFLAC ❖ Aim Management ❖ American Airlines ❖ Bridgestone/Firestone ❖ Cigna Healthcare ❖ ClubCorp ❖ Daryl Flood Movers ❖ Direct Energy Marketing ❖ Duke Energy ❖ FedEx ❖Hillcrest Hospital ❖ Lands' End ❖ Mannatech ❖ Mount Clemens Hospital ❖ PFSweb ❖ Professional Services Incorporated ❖ SalesLink ❖ Security Finance ❖ Social Security Administration ❖Texas Guarantee Student Loan ❖ Tower Group, International

He is consistently ranked #1 in conference and keynote evaluations and comments as follows are common:

> *"He was fantastic! Very well organized."*
>
> *"David Cottrell was very energetic and presented the material in a clear and concise manner."*
>
> *"Very dynamic speaker who positively addressed a lot of issues that we deal with daily."*
>
> *"Dynamic, knowledgeable and passionate about the subject matter. Very smooth presentation."*
>
> *"Thanks so much for investing the time and resources necessary to provide this training."*
>
> *"I loved all of it! Even with over 20 years of management experience, it was very beneficial and I picked up some important tips."*

To book David Cottrell for your next conference or in-house event, please contact:

Barbara Bartlett
CornerStone Leadership Institute
888-789-LEAD (5323)
www.davidcottrell.com

Acknowledgements

Over the years, I have been blessed with some wonderful mentors. My success has been molded and formed by those who always seem to have the time to listen and the wisdom to share.

I thank the following people for being my mentors:

Alice Adams, Paul Damoc, Ty Deleon, Louis Kruger, Mark Layton, Joe Miles, Wallace Moorehand, Tony Van Roekel, and Tod Taylor.

I am also grateful to the people whose expertise made *Monday Morning Leadership* a reality: Alice Adams and Juli Baldwin — my editors. Defae Weaver — book designer, Keith Crabtree — cover designer and Barbara Bartlett — my assistant who held everything together while this book was being completed.

To all of you whom I have named, please accept my deepest thanks.

To each person who reads this book, best wishes as you become a positive role model, mentor, and friend for the people around you.

Other CornerStone Leadership Books:

Becoming the Obvious Choice is a roadmap showing each employee how they can maintain their motivation, develop their hidden talents and become the best $9.95

Listen Up, Leader! Ever wonder what employees think about their leaders? This book tells you the seven characteristics of leadership that people will follow. $9.95

175 Ways to Get More Done in Less Time has 175 really, really good suggestions that will help you get things done faster…and usually better. $9.95

Memos to Managers are sincere and powerful messages to managers from unusual sources. This unique book is loaded with real world leadership lessons. $9.95

The Manager's Coaching Handbook is a practical guide to improve performance from your superstars, middle stars and falling stars. $9.95

Leadership…Biblically Speaking is a guide on how to apply the leadership lessons from the Bible to today's leadership challenges. $17.95

Birdies, Pars & Bogeys: Leadership Lessons From The Links makes an excellent gift for the golfing executive. Zig Ziglar praises it as "concise, precise, insightful, inspirational, informative, and just plain common sense." $12.95

Listen UP, Sales & Customer Service is written from the perspective of a customer who cares enough to tell you the truth. This book maps a step-by-step pathway to long-lasting customer relationships. $9.95

136 Effective Presentation Tips is a powerful handbook providing 136 practical, easy to use tips to make every presentation a success. $9.95

Listen UP, Teacher…You Are Making a Difference is a motivational and inspirational message to teachers written from the perspective of students. It provides teachers a unique look at the impact that they have on students. $9.95

Sticking to It: The Art of Adherence is a dynamic guide to help you and your team achieve more. It provides practical tips for executing your personal and team strategies. $9.95

To order any of these books,
contact Cornerstone Leadership Institute
at 888.789.LEAD (5323) or visit
www.cornerstoneleadership.com

Recommended Resources for Additional Study:

Drivers and Passengers
Listen Up, Leader! Pay Attention, Improve and Guide

Keep the Main Thing the Main Thing
Walk the Talk…And Get The Results You Want

Escape from Management Land
Memos To: Managers. Leadership Lessons to Read, Learn From, and Apply

The 'Do Right' Rule
Ethics 4 Everyone: The Handbook for Integrity-Based Business Practices

Hire Tough
The Manager's Coaching Handbook: A Practical Guide To Improving Employee Performance

Do Less or Work Faster
175 Ways to Get More Done in Less Time

Buckets and Dippers
180 Ways to Walk the Recognition Talk

Enter the Learning Zone
Becoming the Obvious Choice: A Guide to Your Next Opportunity

To order these recommended resources call:
1-888-789-LEAD (5323)

☑ **Yes! Please send me extra copies of** *Monday Morning Leadership!*

1-100 copies $12.95 each   101-499 copies $11.95   500+ copies $10.95 each

Monday Morning Leadership   ___ copies X _____   =$_____

Additional Leadership Development Books

Listen Up, Leader!   ___ copies X $9.95   =$_____

Walk the Talk … And Get The Results You Want ___ copies X $21.95   =$_____

The Manager's Coaching Handbook   ___ copies X $9.95   =$_____

"Memos" To: Managers   ___ copies X $9.95   =$_____

Ethics 4 Everyone   ___ copies X $9.95   =$_____

175 Ways to Get More Done in Less Time   ___ copies X $9.95   =$_____

180 Ways to Walk the Recognition Talk   ___ copies X $9.95   =$_____

136 Effective Presentation Tips   ___ copies X $9.95   =$_____

Becoming the Obvious Choice   ___ copies X $9.95   =$_____

Leadership Development Package   ___ packs   X $99.95   =$_____

Shipping and Handing $_____

Subtotal $_____

Sales Tax (8.25%-TX Only) $_____

Total (U.S. Dollars Only)   **$_____**

Shipping and Handling Charges

Total $ Amount	Up to $50	$51-$99	$100-$249	$250-$1199	$1200-$3000	$3000+
Charge	$5	$8	$16	$30	$80	$125

Name _____ Job Title _____

Organization_____ Phone _____

Shipping Address _____ FAX _____

Billing Address _____ Email _____

City _____State _____ Zip _____

☐ Please invoice (Orders over $200) Purchase Order Number (If applicable)

Charge Your Order: ☐ Mastercard   ☐ Visa   ☐ American Express

Credit Card Number _____ Exp. Date_____

Signature _____
☐ Check Enclosed (Payable to CornerStone Leadership)

Fax	**Mail**	**Phone**
972.274.2884	**P.O. Box 764087**	**888.789-5323**
	Dallas, TX 75376